# *If Dreams Come True*

by

# *Noorah Deen*

author HOUSE®

*AuthorHouse™ UK Ltd.*
*500 Avebury Boulevard*
*Central Milton Keynes, MK9 2BE*
*www.authorhouse.co.uk*
*Phone: 08001974150*

*First published by AuthorHouse  10/29/2009*

*ISBN: 978-1-4490-1298-4 (sc)*

*This book is printed on acid-free paper.*

*To my family, thank you!*

# Table of Contents

# Words

A celebration of words
In a weird world.

A celebration of emotion
And passion without fashion.

Deep elusive feelings
Blended into obsessive thoughts

Flourishing the beautiful mind with inspiration
And constant creation with absolute joys in the soul.

Noorah Deen

# College Days

College days joyful.
Hopeful highlights to success,
And expected dreams for all of us,
As we sauntered through our class works
Carefully but not delightfully.
As usual, lost in my thought,
 Keats's famous line
Came to my mind:
"Beauty lies in the eyes of the beholder",
And Coleridge wrote:
"Water, water, everywhere,
But, alas, not a drop to drink".
I can even visualize the scene:
In the middle of the vast ocean
There is not any clean drinking water
As everywhere is surrounded by salted sea water.
Clear and vivid pictures came to my mind
 With indelible meaning.
The words just flashed in front of my eyes
As if it was yesterday.
Books and copybooks spreading all over the desks
And the open pages brought undesired memories.
Coleridge, Chaucer, Jane Austen,
"Sense and Sensibility"
"A House for Mr. Biswas".
All bring tears of boredom.
Dull classes, silly teachers,
Lazy pupils, boring atmosphere.
Feeling restless and talkative
Only Shakespeare could keep us awake
With his lively intelligence
And dramatic plays:
"Macbeth"
"Othello"
"The Merchant of Venice"
"Hamlet".
Famous plays in different ways, indeed.
They hold our attention constantly
Without our eyes wavering from the pages.
Suspense and shock unfolded,
In dramatic scenarios
And pessimistic outcome.

## (II)

A genius for writing
Immortal words captured in lively scenes
As in "King Lear"
When Gloucester's sorrows became evident
 When he lamented in despair:
"As flies to wanton boys
Are we to the gods,
They kill us for their sports",
While King Lear himself
Was having a miserable time
Coping with the cruelties of his daughters.
After obtaining his wealth and property,
Both daughters became very nasty towards him.
This is truly human nature
And Shakespeare did a marvelous job
In emphasizing the greediness
And selfishness of mankind.
All those stories came flashing through my mind,
Bringing back memories of carefree days
Filled with laughter and mischief
Together with all the class mates.
Not even when Keats cried about his sadness,
Or when he sauntered lazily
Through his solitude
Did that diminish our joys of living.
Shakespeare brought us great delights.
Our eyes wide open
No time to feel sleepy,
Visualizing Gloucester's despair in the horrible weather
Experiencing King Lear's feeling of shock and pain,
As heavy rain pouring outside
Drowning their tears into magnanimous sorrows,
While our class continued peacefully.

# *Feeling*

The feeling is always there.
Unconsciously wrapped up warmly
In velvet pink ribbons.
I don't want to untie it
For fear it would disappear.
Like lightning, it strikes me straight into the heart,
Sending multi-colored bubbles through my soul.
A profound emotion of love being shared and nurtured.
True love and true feelings
Between two hearts forever bound into one,
Body and soul together.
My heart cries joyously,
A sweet and tantalizing whisper in my ears.
The most beautiful sound I have ever heard.
The most wonderful words I have ever longed to hear
And it is a love song
Coming straight from your heart
With true special words sung
Just for me
Welcome into my world
Welcome into my heart.
Love
To care and to share,
Eyes full of promises and hopes,
Wanting only the very best for each other.
Love runs wild,
 Love runs wide,
As we smile,
 Millions of miles.
Apart we are together
Separate, we are united.

# *Mahebourg*

Mahebourg
Endless dreams
Unwiped memories
Unseen treasures.

Blue-Bay
Endless blue
Unlimited beauty
Unseen reality.

**"Mahebourg: Endless Blue"**

White beach
Soft sand
Clear crystal water
A blue reflection.

So much temptation
For a lazy
And carefree swim
In the open ocean.

Noorah Deen

Fun in the sun
Enjoying a lively picnic
Amidst great entertainment
And loud laughter.

Some dancing on "sega" vibes
While others whistle some tunes
To get the show going
And the excitement exploding.

Beating on the drums
While lots of rhum is flowing around,
Soon they are lost in great giggles
And are riddled with joys.

Some have brought their "biryani" food
Some have brought fried noodles
Or some fresh fish curry smelling delicious
While others are busy making a braii.

A good opportunity
A daily reality
To enjoy some delicious
And tasty mouth-watering special menus.

The people of Mauritius
Loves to spend wonderful times
By the sea-side
Alongside the "filaos" trees.

Some sellers are busy selling ice-cream
Some are selling coconuts or peanuts
While others prefer to sell mango and pine-apple salads
Mixed with chilies.

## (II)

What a temptation?
What a revelation?
What a divine taste
Of pure Mauritian tradition?

The smell is unbelievable
The taste incredible
The atmosphere just superb
The ambiance unimaginable.

With all the dancing
And singing going on
Nobody is ready to go home
Everyone seems oblivious to time.

Mahebourg
My beautiful town
Cradle of my childhood
And witness of my million dreams.

Carried away by the sweet whispers
Of far away memories
But so much present
In my mind.

I see Mahebourg
The bridge near my house
The river and the sea
On both sides of the road.

Mahebourg
Sauntering along the streets
I see the Chinese shops
"Li – Cho", "Kong", "Pac Soo"

All bring tender memories
Of carefree childhood
Innocent soul
And excited wishes.

(II)

**(III)**

Mahebourg
Enchanted in the Indian Ocean
Reveals its true panorama
Across a spectacular foam of waves.

Mahebourg
Pointe -Aux- Canons
The Monument of the Slaves
Naval museum displaying the various battles.

Battle of Grand-Port
The General warriors
Willoughby
And Duperre.

Pointe -des-Regates
A relaxing corner
For families and friends
Admiring the lovely blue sea.

Mouchoir Rouge
L'Ile-aux-Phares
L'Ile-aux-Aigrettes
Montagne Lion.

Debarcadere
Bateau Roche
Pointe-D'Esny
The new bus terminal.

SSR International Airport
Welcomes visitors
With genuine friendliness
And politeness.

Mahebourg
Dressed in its spectacular fashion
Enhanced its eternal beauty
And is forever a temptation.

Mahebourg
Incredible!
Unbelievable!
Unforgettable!

# *Falling In Love*

Some more stars in the sky
Some more birds humming in the trees
Some more music in the air
And love is all around.

Falling in love in wild summer
While everything is in good harmony
While every rose is in perfect joy
Is the most wonderful thing to happen.

**"Are red roses for eternal love?"**

Closing her eyes, she breathes in
The sweetness of yesterday's tenderness
Gorgeous days of cherished memories
Overshadowed by scars of today's pain.

May be she expects too much from love.
May be she expects too much from the person she loves.
May be love does not exist.
May be love is just a fragment of lies and imagination.

Falling in love is so easy.
Finding the right person so difficult
True love is so rare.
Loyalty is such an empty word.

Behind every romantic picture
There is a love story
Behind every love story
There is a broken heart.

And behind every broken heart
There are pain and tears for always.
Dreams never come true.
They are just pure irrelevant fantasies.

Today's dreams become tomorrow's sorrows.
Bemused and bewitched,
Incapable of rational thoughts,
Only fools let romance take control of their lives.

Love is passion
Love is obsession
Love is insanity
Love is reality.

# I Wished I Could Fly!

Long and lovely night
Feeling happy at your sight
Shedding your diamond-colored lights
Across the canvas of the blue sky
I wished I could fly!

Summer nights!
Sweet delights!
A big rounded moon smiling
And sailing across a warm cloudless sky.
I wished I could fly!

White-colored velvet moon
Sparkling brightly and tenderly.
Sweet-honeyed moon
Wrapped in its fragile cocoon
It disappears too soon.

Beautiful nights
Wonderful flights
Across the unbounded universe.
Time seems suspended
Far away and always.

Spread across the ocean mighty waves
The night's giant wings,
And angels are busy singing
God's worthy praises
As their voices raises

Up in the sky
I wished I could fly!
Witnessing nature's unlimited beauty
O Mighty Night!
O Magnificent Delight!

O Noble night!
O Creation! O Beauty!
Pure and silky tapestry of colors.
If you have not been there
We would still have been working.

Nights and days
Everywhere and everyday,
Everybody keeps on working and rushing with a busy schedule.
Grateful you are among us,
Giving us time to sleep and to dream.

Mysterious nights
Multi-colored flights
The gentle whistling of the breeze
And the glittering stars in the sky,
I wished I could fly!

Far away some dogs start barking furiously,
Breaking the night's sweet spell viciously.
My heart stops singing.
In silence I hear the bell ringing,
And I realized that fate is catching up with me.

Some memories never fade, is it too late?
Some tears never dry, is it time to cry?
Some hearts never mend, would I be hurt again?
In front of pain and disillusion
O Sweet night! Give me a reply…

Bright, Bubbly and Beautiful
O Mighty night!
O Sweet delight!
Rose above the hills some melodious voices,
Glorifying the Lord, who is full of Mercy and Wisdom.

In this spiritual and peaceful atmosphere,
A universe filled with stars and hopes,
In this everlasting beauty
Like some merry butterflies
I wished I could fly!

Down the memory lane
Came thorny thoughts insane
And from the ashes of my wild and sweet dreams
I heard some bitter screams.
I learned to fly on broken wings...

# Time Of Eternity...

When comes time of adversity
Till rose sublime eternity
Then flooded cold reality
And there is no serenity.

Life
Just like a knife
Cuts through ruthlessly
And heedlessly.

Painful walks
Heavy loads
Endless roads
Broad and abroad.

Life
Like a volcano
Molten lava pierces inside
Knocks and blows throw you aside

Then comes reality
Time of Eternity...
Where is destiny?
When there is no generosity?

# *For Every...*

For every storm
There is a rainbow.

For every sunset
There is a sunrise.

**Rays Spread Across The Purple Pink Horizon**

For every dawn
There is sunshine.

For every thorn
There is a rose.

For every dream
There is a hope.

 For every broken heart
There is a joyful song.

And love comes only
After a very long drought season.

Hopes run high happily
Sublime joys dancing merrily.

Sparkling rays spread across
A simmering sunshine over a vivid golden horizon,

Welcome with open arms
Inviting happiness to join the feast.

With the least hesitation
Without notification

Happiness made its way to her heart
On a spectacular rising beat.

Slowly, her world comes alive
Giving rise to the most beautiful sunrise.

# A Poet's Life

O time of Greatness!
O time of Sweetness!
Why have you vanished into thin air?
When I needed you most?
When I felt truly lost?

I dreamed about a poet's life.
It cuts through like a knife,
Leaving behind a wrecked body
And a confused mind
With hopeless signs.

All poets are sensitive
But rarely positive.
Negative thoughts
Restless soul
Careless walks.

Whispered talks
Confused thoughts
Always looking for something which rarely exists.
They sense life truly and fully.
Fate played an important part of it.

O Sensitiveness! When you hold us in your grip,
O Truthfulness! When our soul is cruelly ripped,
A poet feels life more sadly
Sorrow deepens his restless soul
For tomorrow holds no promises for him.

Feeling like an alien in this world
Out of time and out of place
No craving desire for a palace
He finds peace and solace
In his solitude.

A genius gift for writing.
Through pain and witnessing the suffering of others,
Inspiration comes slowly and truly.
Reality becomes more real
And words come flowing down like "Victoria Falls".

**Words Cascade Down Like Victoria Falls**

# While...

While I was sleeping in a dark cold room,
Some images crept in silently
And dreams came flooding freely.
My mind blooming in colors.

Wandering in a garden of roses,
Wearing a long white dress of lovely laces
And dancing sweetly to the soft breezes,
Smelling each rose ardently.

My feet barely touched the ground.
Feeling light and carefree,
My soul sings happily
Rhymes of ancient times.

My mind wandering off to far away places.
My soul roamed to large spacious green pastures.
My eyes forever lost in this enchanted surrounding
And my arms wide open to welcome this peaceful scenery.

Feeling the quietness deep in my heart
Sensing that nature is in peace with herself
I just feel happy and light-hearted.
No worries and no pains.

Wanting to leave everything behind,
The glamorous societies
The false lime-lights
The cold and arrogant politeness.

The lies and all glitters
All shows and glib talks
They are masquerade and pretence
In honeyed sentences.

In a world of foes
And hypocrisy
One would prefer
To be alone.

# Time

Great is her pain
As she walks in the rain.

Tumbling along the lane
Slowly, she goes insane.

She realizes love is pain
Love is no gain.

Her body shaken with fears
And her eyes full of tears,

As it rains inside her heart
Draining all her hopes away.

In downpours
Outbursts.

She feels like sleeping
Her eyes feel like weeping.

Time slipped by painfully
As she continued roaming hopefully.

# *Botswana*

Dreaming of Africa
Surrounded by Botswana
Her sweet home.

Leaving all unhappy memories behind
Life seems more cheerful.
Botswana offers peace and friendliness.

Since the death of her beloved mother
Botswana has been the place she can run
To wipe away all tears and sorrows

Longing for a simple way of life
No crazy for fashion and glittering.
Botswana is the home she has been looking for.

Gaborone, an ordinary city in rush hours
No need for sophistication and lime-lights
Devoid of any pretence and masquerade.

Botswana's Coat-of- Arms and its National Flag
Proudly symbolized peace
And prosperity.

Botswana, Sweet Botswana
A dream comes true
A reason to believe in love.

No luxurious skyscrapers.
Not much entertainment around
But peace and friendliness of its people compensate all that.

Botswana, my second home
My quiet refuge
Fused in serene wilderness.

African Mall, Main Mall
 Broadhurst, Mokolodi.
River Walk, Game City.

Busy Botswana
Business Botswana
Beautiful Botswana.

David Livingstone in his tombstone
Had his soul buried in Kelobeng
While he was living his dreams there.

"Khotla" meetings animated,
Gospel songs filled the warm summer air
While the drivers of the "combi" taxi speed on recklessly.

Tuck shops, mealie-meal
Cabbage, mopane worms,
"Magwinya", "seswa", all delicious food, indeed.

Soon Batswana welcomes the "Mantshwabisi" race
The Toyota Kalahari Desert Race
With excitement and joys.

Wide Wild Botswana
Carrying its flag proudly in this vast wilderness
The government fighting hard to bring prosperity.

Mokolodi
Gaborone Game Reserve
Lion's Park

Kasane, Ghanzi, Maun,
Kalahari Desert, Okavango Delta
All aspired feelings of laughter and respect.

**Lion King Looking Sad and Lonely Behind the Fence**

Wild beast enjoying the summer feast
Lions, elephants, zebras, rhinoceros, and giraffes.
All roaming lazily around.

**The Powerful Elephant Of Kasane**

Searching for green pastures
But nature offers only dried leaves
Alas, no rain, no water.

An ostrich couple
Roaming around in peace with their chicks
While some baboons are busy jumping from branch to branch.

**A Happy Ostrich Couple enjoying the summer**

Peace blended into nature
The surrounding looked more exotic than ever
Healing the pain slowly but surely.

Footsteps go lightly and confidently
Throughout the road of Botswana
Wishing happiness to each and every Batswana people.

# *If Dreams Come True...*

Mysterious dreams coming through her deep sleep.
She was swimming in a peaceful and clear water.
All kinds of scenes reflected in a multi-colored mirror.
Beautiful sea filled with numerous colored fish:
"Cordonnier", "Millet", "Karang".
She was swimming among them.
Happiness and peace pour into her heart
And the feeling cannot be described,
For it is too precious and rare.
She flows with the water
Enjoying every minute of it
While her favorite fish follow her
In a swirl of ballet dancing
And numerous incredible circus.

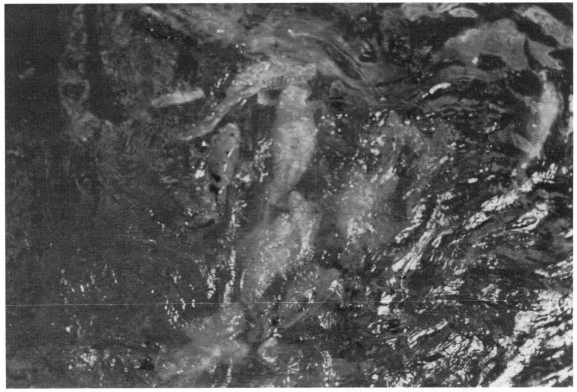

**"Lovely Fish Unite Together In A Peaceful Swim"**

She continued her journey
As another dream crept in joyfully.
Suddenly she saw a lovely huge plane
Parked in front of her house
Waiting for her to take off.
It has got red and blue designs on its surface.
Very often, she dreams about huge planes in the sky.
Suddenly, she is in New-York
Busy admiring the glamorous shops.
Carefree walks
In broad lime-lights
As if she is in Broadway.
And then another unexpected dream made its appearance
Through the journey of her deep sleep.

## (II)

She was in a huge building, together with Oprah Winfrey
And some other ladies,
There were lots of lovely clothes, with beautiful colors,
Some were light pink, yellow, green,
There are also some small 'angora' jerseys and tops.
She was admiring all of them.
Then Oprah approached her
And told her to choose which one she wanted.
Seeing her hesitation, she chose one for her.
It was a long pale yellow dress with straps-like- cross.
She told her that she and her staff
Have put beads all over the dress.
When Oprah asked her to try it on,
She could not believe her ears.
She took the dress happily.
It fits her perfectly, close to the body curve.
She was feeling so shy to come in front of Oprah.
But then, Oprah herself came towards her
And guessed that she liked the dress.
It was really the most beautiful dress she has ever seen.
Then Oprah said to her staff:
"What loss to one is gain to another"
Everyone was surprised that she got the dress.
When she woke up in the morning,
She was thinking about that incredible short episode

When she was in the company of the famous Oprah.
May be it was just an unreal fairy-tale
To keep her dreams alive and real,
As she could not believe she has dreamed about Oprah Winfrey,
The famous American talk-show queen.
The dream is so clear and vivid that she can still visualize it.

## (III)

Another time, she dreamed she is on her way to America.
She was busy preparing a small suitcase.
Her mother was together with her in the room
And she was looking very happy.
Then she was at the airport.
While she was in the queue to board the plane,
She realized suddenly she has forgotten her passport.
She was very upset and worried
She realized she must go back home and look for the passport
Because the authorities would not allow her to get on the plane.
The dream ended there …
And the most amazing thing is that she could still see the plane
But for sure she never boarded it.
That kind of dream of visiting America always came to haunt her.
She just wondered why.
Excited hopes
Wonderful promises.
Such scenes coming frequently in her dreams,
Creating a sense of peace and happiness.

## (IV)

Dreams come and go all through the nights
Keeping her company as her faithful knights.
Part of her life...
Part of her inner soul...
They are her golden treasures for future reference.
Holding them tightly locked,
For fear they would disappear,
Like bubbles in the cloud
Leaving her empty
And thirsty for her lost
And loyal companions.
Her dreams help her to go through life
Ardently and confidently
Bringing hopes on a joyful note.
Living her dreams alive and "on live",
Every scene is remembered vividly,
Every emotion is felt heartily,
While an inner voice advised quietly:
"Hold on to your dreams fiercely.
Believe in them
Fight for them
Never give up.
If you dream it
You will reach it"
For up in the sky
As she flies with golden wings
Melodies ring in her ears.
Bringing tears of joys
To her restless soul.
But another voice whispered dreamily:
"If only dreams come true
Your world would change
From black to blue".

# A Real World...

They can feel it in their heart.
They can see it in their dreams.
They can live it in their world.
Life must go on.
The show must continue
Whatever the cost
Whatever the price.
Crying for the loss of their loved ones,
They know their tears would never dry
Because the warmongers
And the criminals
Are enjoying full support
And protection.
The killings go unnoticed,
While the people are bleeding
In pain and despair.
Defenceless and hopeless
They are at the mercy of the war criminals.
Living in a real world
With real people
And knowing all the agony they are going through each day,
A life of torture and suffering
And humiliations.
Convinced that nobody would come to their rescue
Because they are just considered
As an unwanted burden better to get rid of
As they do not possess any wealth or resources.
They try to make a living in the war zone area.
Tortured and killed ruthlessly
The warmongers continue the massacre
With complete freedom to act.
No justice means no peace.
Prayers bring serenity to many broken hearts.
While the atrocities rage on in complete indifference.

**(II)**

Faith brings determination and strength
To many desperate souls,
Because as usual,

Full of arrogance and defiance,
The murderers claim victory too soon on defenceless lives.
In the dark corner of their world,
Pain has strengthened their faith
To fight against their unfortunate fate.
There is nothing fake in their world.
Just pure brutal deaths,
On hungry and helpless civilians.
Determined never to give up,
Wiping their tears hopefully and courageously,
They make their way to the church
Leaving the ruthless and the powerful warmongers
To plan another strategy.
They finally realize that they must rely on themselves
And their faith to fight for their rights
And put an end to this insane massacre
On innocent and defenceless people,
Such as the Rwanda genocide,
The Bosnian massacre
The conflict in the Democratic of Congo
And so many other killings still going on unabated.

# Here Comes The Rain...

Picking up some "morula" fruits which have fallen carelessly on the ground
At "Sanitas Garden" in Gaborone on a bright Sunday morning,
Surrounded by all the lovely roses
And beautiful hibiscus,
Of all colors and shapes.
Sweet whispers.
Fabulous fragrance.
Gorgeous colors casting their magic spell in the air.
Divine truth of beauty!
Soon she made her way home,
Leaving behind her the quiet and peaceful scene.
The blue beautiful sky
With white snow flakes of cloud hanging around,
Watching lazily the golden shining sun
Spreading its majestic wings
Over the vast incredibly lovely panorama.
All of a sudden, heavy drops of rain
Started pouring noisily
Across the window pane.
She could see the clear crystal water
Dripping and sizzling
Into small broken-like-diamond pieces.
After a disastrous drought and a dreadful heat,
Rain is always a blessing.
A mercy from God Almighty
And a sure welcome by all of us.
Suddenly, thunders smashed the sky
Into raging and ferocious loud noises,
While lightning split into lines and curves,
Brightening the night as if it is day time.

Thunders continued to roar furiously
While rain kept falling madly and happily,
Bringing smiles and hopes to all of us.
Trees and dams welcome this downpour,
While plants blossom alive
And all the animals breathe a sign of relief,
As everybody is truly rejoiced by this spectacular picture.
The farmers have big smiles.
Indeed, ploughing and harvesting look very promising.
Even the donkeys look happy,
While grazing around the Molepolole green pasture.

## "A Disastrous Drought"

After confronting drought for such a long time
And aids epidemic on a large scale
Botswana vows
Not to bow in front of adversity.
More than ever
She stands proud and strong,
Refusing to show weakness
And cowardice.
Botswana, the shining diamond of Africa

The courageous smile of its people
The strength of its "Kalahari Desert"
The eternal beauty of the "Okavango Delta"
The "Tsodilo Hills",
"Makgadikgadi Pans"
And 'The Chobe National Park'.
Together, let us make Botswana,
The land of diamonds,
To be the success sparkling story of Africa.

# Wonder Words...

A world filled with wonder words.
A wonder world filled with magic words.
Blank pages become alive and worth reading.
Black ink fused into meaningful descriptions,
Giving life to millions of lively letters.
Blue ink adds colors to a dull scenery.
Mighty and Magnificent Words
Which are choreographed together
To bring out vivid and clear pictures
Of pain and joys,
And enlarge the frame
To a display of emotion and feelings.
Some says reading about the suffering of others
Is very boring and a waste of time,
While others appreciate the very depth
Of those emotions felt daily by any one of us
To enrich their own lives
And learn valuable lessons.
As for those who are going through a life of hardship,
They can understand the fact
That from those painful moments,
They can come out a better person
And not a bitter person.
Their suffering strengthen their determination
To see peace and justice prevailing around
And happiness for everyone.
In a world where foes are busy spreading chaos
To justify their insane and greedy agendas,
Beautiful and powerful words have become her only hopes
To repel violence and injustice
Because the cowards lie, bribe and manipulate things
Behind the scenes.

No swords are needed.
No missiles or cluster bombs
Because these words are not weapons of mass destruction
But they are weapons of mass awakening
To a beautiful and just world for each one of us.
The defenseless should feel safe every second of the day.
The vulnerable should live without fear.
The children should feel loved and secured.
The women should feel strong and confident
And we must give the opportunity to everyone to believe by our actions
That happiness, peace and brotherhood do exist
In this cruel and unjust world.
Giant words!
Monumental meaning!
Valuable treasures!
Absolute Truth!

# She Imagines...

She imagines love to be
As pure and clear as crystal
Shining colorless
Without a dent.
A perfect love.

That kind of love
Which is filled with honey,
Laughter,
Devotion,
And complete trust.

Sweet mesmerizing feelings
Invading thoughts
Of a restless soul.
With true promises
For a happy tomorrow.

She dreamed about love
At first sight
Bringing sparkling lights
Into the dark nights.
At the sight of hope and faith.

Romance grows steadily,
Blossoming into little timid smiles.
Tender, rare and everlasting.
But O how beautiful!
And special it is!

## Lovely Orchids Blossom Into Attractive Flagrance

Brushing shyness aside,
Love made its way
At full speed
With great confidence
And a cordial approach.

Knocking her down
On a bed of roses
In a garden of dazzling colors.
Happy spirits running freely
Butterflies bouncing merrily

While music whispered romantic melodies,
Soon, she was flying high
Above the landscape
And the mountains
Across the vast ocean.

In her dream,
Slowly and surely,
She felt she was being lifted
Like a precious doll
With a joyful soul.

Flying light and higher
Into the invisible space,
She left the mischievous world behind,
Refusing to look back at the past
Which she really wants to erase.

Enjoying every second
Of this beautiful and carefree flight,
Love followed her faithfully.
The peaceful cloud becomes
The roof of her dreamed house.

The lovely moon becomes
The shelter of her happiness,
And the glittering stars turn out
To be her trusted
And loyal companions.

Unwilling to wake up
Refusing to come down on earth
Preferring the dream to continue forever
She felt very much enticed
To her glorious surrounding.

Birds joined in the feast
Angels dancing dreamily
To sweet promises
Of tomorrow's delights
And far away flights...

**"Birds Celebrating Her Happiness"**

# *Stars In The Eyes...*

Looking for attention
Seeking attraction
Turning into obsession.

The single
Mingles in the crowd
Cheering to loud laughter.

Stars in the eyes
Dimples in the cheeks
With sparkling smiles.

Firm determination
Final resolution
Wild expectation.

Searching for Mr. Right
She meets Mr. Gangster
In a web of deceits.

On the look out for fun
She runs straight into the trap
Of guns, drugs and alcohol.

Instead of finding a handsome hero
She finds dangerous heroin
And cocaine.

Living in their world
She starts implementing
Their lifestyles.

Tattoos on the backside
Navel pierced
Unravels a carefree spirit.

Hanging on to her wings
Brings her closer to her goal
Sings a joyous soul.

As she clings
To her dreams
Of happiness ever after.

The flight continues in delight
As she glides
Through the soft cocoon of cloud.

And as she climbs up
Into the mysterious unknown
With well-known consequences

Soon, she loses sight of reality
As she drugs herself
In this make-believe world of ecstasy.

She is looking for a tender and sweet soul
But, instead, she finds furious thunder awaiting her
Causing disruption in her life.

She has taken the fast lane
For a speed crack
And mandrax.

High on crystal met
Rave and tik
She finally reaches the end of her road.

Her eyes refuse to open
As she slips in a state of confusion
And utter despair.

Blurred vision
Risky mission
Empty dreams.

High music sound crashed
On a loud tempo beat
As the party heats up on a high vibe.

And dancing a jive
On super live
She is full of life.

Walking in a trance
Dancing in a frenzy
Going slowly crazy...

Overdose
Over the top
Down the slope.

On the path of self-destruction,
Complete confusion
Final destination.

Being in a daze
Dazzled her spirit
And spoils her soul.

Magic spell vanished.
Her world collapsed
In tragic end.

A young and lifeless body
With shattered dreams
Screams an innocent voice.

# Tsodilo, Mountain Of The Gods.

The blue and clear sky
With white flake of cloud spreading around
Watches lazily the golden shining sun
Stretching its majestic wings
Across the vast and incredibly lovely panorama.

Bright, bubbly and peaceful
The atmosphere is just perfect
To welcome "Tsodilo",
Mountain of the Gods
And master of the landscape.

Rose above the desert scenery
A landmark in Botswana
"Tsodilo" has been chosen
As a World Heritage Site.
What a sacred sight!

A monument full of life
Which strives to bring
The true beauty of nature
As it is dressed in its simple
And ordinary fashion of everyday.

Indeed, with much pride
And confidence,
"Tsodilo" evokes cultural inspiration
National satisfaction
And eternal jubilation.

# In Silence ... With A Smile

Arrogance
Selfishness
Nastiness
Are all blended into human beings
To make a beautiful face
And an attractive smile.
Burning jealousy brings another kind of sickness to the heart.
In silence… with a smile
So many things can be done to harm someone.
Never trust a smile.
Never trust a word delivered with honey
When the heart is full of poisonous venom.
Hypocrisy with diplomacy
Such a coward act.
She never utters a word.
She keeps a complete silence.
This means you never know what there is in her heart,
And what her feelings are.
Just a frozen smile on her artificial face,
Like a plastic flower with no genuine perfume.
In her desire to be more clever than anybody,
She forgets she has a see-through face.
Every expression can be read easily
Every gesture can be interpreted immediately.
Cold and calculated,
Behind her sweet words lies a desire to get things done her own way,
In a clever and subtle manner,
Without arousing any suspicions about her true nature.
Behind her gorgeous smile hides vengeance and revenge.
Behind her kind words lies a desire to manipulate any situation

To her benefit and advantage,
And create division and antagonism to prevail
In order to have full control over everyone and everything.
One thing is for sure
Her see-through face can be read like an open book.
She really thinks her rude manners and back-biting would go unnoticed
Because she considers herself too much smart
And others too stupid and dumb to understand her calculated plot.
She causes trouble between friends and neighbours
Then sits back and enjoys the drama,
Pretending she does not know what is going on.
When she talks you cannot hear her voice
She talks so quietly and smiling at the same time,
But her intentions are only evil and nasty.
She goes around telling lies about others
To make people believe she is the perfect angel.
In silence… with a smile
She causes hatred, division, and destruction.
She talks to you so sweetly and calmly.
She holds you in a close hug
Showing you affection and care,
Then in silence… with a smile
In a split second,
She stabs you into pieces.
What a pity human nature hides so much venom and hatred.
But the truth is jealousy and nastiness can only destroy yourself
Because those you try to harm and cause pain
Would always rise and shine in honor and dignity!

# Mavis And Masego

Mavis
Masego
What do they have in common?
Well, not only do they carry the same letter"M" in their names,
But they are also H.I.V positive.
A situation which has obliged them to stay away from society.
Ashamed of their status
Ignored by their relatives and friends,
They prefer to stay alone,
Out of the crowd
And out of the curious gazes.
Two lonely women with two different
But painful stories.
Since the day they have both decided
To take a test at "Tebelopele"
Their dreams have been completely shattered.
It was the darkest day of their lives,
With a quick end to a hopeful tomorrow
And a joyful future.
Sitting under the "mopane" tree
The two women reflect on their past.
Masego is still wondering for the million times
How could this happen to her?
She has been too naïve to trust that man
Who has come to cause havoc in her life.
Masego, a mother of two still cannot believe
She has been contaminated by her husband
Whom she has foolishly trusted.
What would happen to her beloved children, wondered Masego…
Her sweet Andile and Kabelo
Her two favorite and loyal angels.
She refuses to think about her children
Becoming orphans at a young age.
Masego wears her sunglasses always
So that nobody can see her pain and her tears.

## (II)

As for Mavis, she was raped one night
When she came from a party.
Walking alone in the bush,
She was grasped suddenly by a stranger
Who brutally assaulted her and raped her.
No one could hear her cries of pain
In the silence of the night!
Only the darkness can witness her utter confusion
And her bewildered trauma
As the man disappeared in the night
Taking his secret with him.
Since then, she has regular nightmares
As she still carries the scars of that awful and traumatic event.
But Mavis refuses to give up on her dreams
To become a top model.
She would never allow pain and self-guilt
To control her life.
Both women know they must face a life of loneliness
And terrible hardship.
Marginalized by the society at large
They must constantly be on their guard
To avoid open condemnation
And self-recrimination,
Because as soon as you make your status public
Society immediately points fingers at you for being a perverse
And a burden for the family and friends.
But both women decide to face life with courage and determination.
They refuse to sit down all day
Twiddling their fingers and doing nothing worthwhile
Or moving from "shebeen" to bars
Swallowing their pain in "chibuku" or beers and wine,
And destroying their self- esteem
And the little hope they have.
Instead, both Mavis and Masego dedicated their time
To help others, especially those affected by H.I.V Aids.
They make sure they are present on every first December
To commemorate' WORLD AIDS DAY' in a fruitful and dynamic way
In order to bring acute awareness to each and everyone
So that they become responsible and accountable for their actions.
Both women work very hard to deliver their message loud and clear.

# (III)

They would like to see everyone making a personal commitment
To reduce the Aids pandemic in a very significant manner in Botswana.
Due to their dedication to uplift the welfare of the community
And their own perseverance to bring success to themselves
Both women stand tall and courageous in front of adversity.
They strive to bring the notion of "Ubuntu" not only on Africa Day
But on each and every day for everyone to feel special and caring.
Their wish is to rise and shine
In front of all the negative and wicked attitude directed towards them
And others who have to live the same predicament.
Since both women have started the anti-retro viral treatment,
They are feeling much better.
Their wish to live longer and make things better for themselves have intensified
And the thirst for happiness has become more acute than ever
Because they believe in a promising tomorrow.
Mavis who has always wanted to be a top model
Has already entered the "Miss H.I.V Positive Living Pageant" contest.
And a few months later
To her complete joys
She is crowned Miss H.I.V Positive.
She promised herself she would bring lots of laughter
And happiness to all those who are suffering in silence.
She decides to create an organization called "MAVIS CARE"
In order to bring relief and real joys to those forgotten members of the society,
Especially the unfortunate children who have been caught up
In this chaos of pain brought by the reckless
And careless behavior of the adults.

## (IV)

As for Masego who has a passion for writing,
She decides to put her pen on paper
And write a biography and a novel.
And finally her struggle to get her novel published comes to an end.
Now she is very proud of herself when she saw her books
On the shelves of the different bookshops in town.
She gives four copies to the National Library of Gaborone
And she is really very happy that now she can provide
A decent living to her two children.
She has got big dreams for her family
And she intends realizing as many as possible.
She strongly believes that behind every dark cloud
There is a silver lining and a multi-colored rainbow,
And she intends keeping her optimism alive.
Due to their self-determination and utmost courage
Both Mavis and Masego have brought great success
And reward in their lives.
And both are very proud to show it off.
"Letlhafula" day is soon coming.
A day of entertainment and joys
Filled with traditional dances and exotic cultures
Which she and her friends would not miss.
They will be there
Dancing on the excited beats
And sharing their happiness with everyone.

# *Click On Happiness*

Do not allow your life to pass you by
While you are still thinking what would be your next steps.
Do not waste your life in futile thoughts
And negative inputs.
Rise and shine in honor
And dignity
Surrounded by the pure glory of God's blessings.
Learn to rise and shine above the pain
For you have a lot to gain.
Do not allow insane acts of others
To pinch you down.
Click on your heart
Downgrade your pain
Download your hopes
Upgrade your happiness.
Delete unnecessary baggage
And any unwanted folders.
Close the files of the past for ever.
Do not be tempted to even get a tiny glimpse of it.
Avoid reminiscences and regrets.
When it comes to the past
Use the word "delete" as much as possible.
Then clear any shadow.
Print in bold and gold uppercase
The word "HAPPINESS"
Font size 70.
Font color pink
Fill color rose.
Textured with large confetti
Sparkled and shimmer.

Click on "HAPPINESS"
And don't look back.
Other virus would try to make their way through
To fill your life with pain and sorrow
But if you stand strong and defiant
No one can destroy you.
Do not look back.
Move forward.
Click on the arrow on the right direction
Follow the path of truth and justice
And you will stand up tall and bright
In the beautiful sunshine
And glory of the day.
Do not allow the lies and the manipulations of others
To darken the path of your dreams.
Do not rewind the tape of your past
To get a preview of what pain is all about.
Do not send it to the recycle bin
Because it would come back and haunt you again.
Just delete and destroy it forever
As swiftly as possible
For your own peace of mind.
Insert clip-art "Fun & Joys"
Across the centre of your life.
Apply auto-format "Colorful"
Insert as Header "JOYS"
And as footer "ALWAYS".
Choose the bright blue highlight for the sentence
"I AM HAPPY"
Engraved and everlasting effect.
Change the page orientation of your life
To the most beautiful and sunny landscape.
Save this profile of your life as "JOYS FOREVER"
Peace for all
And kindness to everyone.

# I Dreamed

I dreamed about a house
Which I can call "My Sweet Home".
It is filled with joys and laughter,
And where harmony, true love
And loyalty prevail each and everyday.
I dreamed about a garden of roses of different colors
Without any thorns
And without any bugs
To spoil its petals.
Only birds and butterflies
Are dancing merrily around,
Fabulous and romantic melodies can be heard around.

**"The Garden of My Dreams – pure purple velvet"**

I dreamed about a sea filled with multi-colored fishes
Without any greedy and hungry sharks swimming around
And which are ready to pounce and tear you into pieces.
Beautiful corals in gorgeous colors
And different shapes coming out nicely
All over the area.

Green weeds looking like velvet pitch spreading around
Inviting for a deep contemplation of nature at its best.
The water is so clear and calm
That you feel like having a peaceful and relaxed swim
Because you know you can feel safe and secure
In this absolute fabulous surrounding.
I dreamed about a land
Covered with green trees and gorgeous flowers.
No pollution to threaten their existence.
No global warming to endanger the species.
No carbon emission to pollute the atmosphere
Nobody causes reckless damage and havoc to our eco-system
Which we will keep safe, clean and green.
A calm lake filled with sparkling water pass by
Through a luscious shining velvet green -colored valley.
Palm trees lining all along
With their majestic leaves enhancing the scenery.
A serene and peaceful atmosphere prevailing around.
Some children playing by in joys and laughter.

## (II)

I dreamed about a country
Where everyone lives in peace and justice
And their rights are respected.
No cluster bombs
No mines to maim and to kill.
There is no fear of diseases and infections
No Ebola fever
No Aids pandemics
No bird's or swine flu
And no virus to cause panic and suffering.
I dreamed about a town
Where everyone is free
And enjoys life in dignity.
No alcohol
No drugs abuse.
Only love, compassion and generosity prevail.
No violence
No revenge
No brutal carnage.
Just happiness and peace for each and everyone.
Am I getting carried away by fairy-tales
Or mankind is really capable of showing these kinds of feelings
And behavior?

# Across The Rainbow

A huge red-orange circle
Rising slowly above the horizon
Like a ball of fire
Ready to burst out with joys.
An early bright morning sunrise
Casting its tender beauty around.
A breath-taking loveliness
Summer sunshine spreading
Across the vast landscape.
A fiery exciting light of rays
Rose high above the horizon.
Hopes sparkling alive.
A new beginning.
Pure tantalizing sweet whispers
Mixed up with a fabulous fragrance
Spread across the green smooth velvet grass
And the wild lovely flowers.
Sublime Unreality!
Divine Truth of Beauty!
Gorgeous colors mingled lovingly together.
Sweet breezes come to tease
The serenity and the magnificent landscape.
Across the rainbow
Came a new lease on life.
Over- flooded with joys
Happiness came pouring in.
Song of joys can be heard around.
The future looks cheerful
Like a wonderful promised land.
My beautiful fairy land welcomes me with open arms
As I rush to cuddle myself in its warm embrace.
Never before have I felt so happy and carefree.
After a long harsh winter
And a terrible storm
Came the rainbow!

# A Lesson To Learn

Writing about love has been an easy task
Not because she knows what love is all about
But because she was living in a quiet
And fantasy world of her own.
So busy reading romances such as "Harlequin",
"Mills & Boon" and "Silhouette" collections,
Which have given her the notion
That love must be a fabulous feeling.
A fantastic escape to a world filled
With pink and red roses,
And a delightful perfume.
Eyes blurred with dreams and fevered expectations,
Romantic candlelight settings
Blended into harmony
In a world where only two people exist.
Love, trust, care, devotion and humour
Are the menus of the day.
Is not that wonderful?
But does love really exist?
Some would say "no",
Because they believe that love is just a fragment of our imagination,
While others would say that love is a mysterious emotion
Which nobody understands
But which everybody experiences.
The truth is love is an emotion created by men and women
In order to decorate their fantasy world.
Living in a false little cozy cocoon of his own
And thinking that nothing is more beautiful than love
Can be the greatest mistake one can make
Because falling in love is very easy
But being in love does not mean
That you are in love with the right person.
Man and woman create love and romance
In order to escape the boredom
And perpetual routine of their lives.

## (II)

They also try to find a way to escape
The harsh realities of every day's troubles
And responsibilities.
In this complete chaos of uncertainties and failures
Men and women want to relate themselves
To the fabulous feeling of being in love
And to convince themselves that love
Brings forever joys and blissful moments,
Forgetting heartbreak and loneliness.
But sooner or later
Love does bring its own pain.
Then solitude becomes the daily escapade
While music becomes the everyday loyal companion.
Hurt in his ego
Lonely in his dreams
In the darkest moment
On the endless avenue of sorrow
Came heartache and tears.
"On my own, once again…"
Says one song.
Another one says:
"Is it time to go our separate ways?"
I am sure anyone can relate to these different melodies:
"A man can tell a thousand lies.
I learned my lesson well."
"You got hurt and you are not the first".
"Love makes you cry".
"Do I listen to my head"
Or do I listen to my heart?"
Heart-breaking songs with special meanings
And with an unforgettable significance.
English, French, and Indian melodies
Golden oldies of glorious times
And blissful moments
Came to fill the empty silence
And the broken heart
Amidst painful memories
And endless dreams.

## (III)

Being in love is such a complicated feeling
If you are in love with the wrong person.
May be for some love at first sight
Has become hate at second sight.
And as for those who have lost love too early
Or have learned to love too late
Do not let disappointment overshadow the beautiful feeling of love.
And for those who have fallen in love
For the wrong reasons
With the wrong person
At the wrong time
And at the wrong place
Then surely a lesson must be learned.
No crush
No lust
Because those feelings do not last forever.
Infatuation brings only disillusion
And hopelessness.
Adultery brings only dishonor
And disaster.
So learn to love wisely
Learn to love sincerely.

# *My Beloved Mother*

We are very proud of you.
And you are very precious to us.
Loving and caring, you showed us ways
To accept our misery bravely.
You dreamed with us.
You struggled for us.
And you never faltered to bring the very best for us.
Even after being a widow
You looked after us with so much care and devotion.
Full of courage and compassion,
You were always ready to help anyone
Without complaining or boasting about it.
You have always given us good advice.
You have always encouraged us to do good deeds around us.
I still remember you told us never to harm anyone
Or cause pain to anybody no matter what happens.
And believe me, mother, I still follow your sound advice.
How can we forget you when you have always been there for us?
You have held our hands firmly and securely
To prevent us from falling into failures.
Your steps grew faster
And your hopes brighter.
And your faith stronger because you have always believed
That tomorrow would be better.
Although you became an orphan at an early age yourself
But you never allowed your own sorrow
To spoil our lives together .
You never gave up.
You never abandoned us to go
And look for a better life for yourself.
Instead, you were completely dedicated
To the well-being of all your children.

## (II)

You became the shadow of our steps
And the only person we would run to
When things went wrong.
How can we forget you, mother?
Our hearts say "Never".
Soon, images creep in painfully,
Lingering eternally on far away memories.
Your silhouette still vivid in my mind.
Your small gestures still clear in my vision.
Your advice still hanging in the air,
And your wise words still ringing in my ears.
I know I can never overcome that great loss
Because the pain and the heartache will never end.
Indeed, we have lost the most precious
And cherished person in the world.
You left us too soon,
Leaving behind you broken hearts
And shattered dreams.
Sadly, we did not have enough time
To show you how grateful we are
And neither the opportunity to look after you
With great care and devotion.
Those who still have their mothers are very lucky,
And they should show respect and honor them.
Remember, the love of a mother is the best love
That a person can receive
Because that love is not tinted with selfishness,
Greed and nasty mischiefs.
Whatever the circumstances, a mother will always give
The best to her children.
Each day passing by
The loneliness becomes unbearable.
Your absence visible
And your presence becomes permanently
The shadow of my thoughts
And your death the regret of my soul.

# The Catwalk Lady

A beautiful babe
With an attractive face
And a gorgeous figure
Lingers her silhouette on the glossy magazine.
Very slim and sexy
She wins the "Miss World" pageant contest
And later becomes a top model.
Free like a bee
On a tree
Parading her beauty on the catwalk
And her sexy curves
And deep cleavage
For everyone to admire
And lust after,
She has the world at her feet.
She makes her jogging daily
And follows her strict diet everyday.
For fear of gaining weight,
She avoids any ice-cream
But she prefers eye cream.
Her life is not simple
Because she must spend her time
Keeping her wrinkles away
And removing the pimples with expensive cream,
Anti-pimple, anti-wrinkle, eyes lift,
Anti-ageing, deep moisturizer.

Plastic surgery
Cosmetic uplifting
The lists go on and on.
For fear she lost her so much coveted place
In this crazy world of fashion and entertainment industry,
She must keep the grand appearance entrance.
She wants to keep only her dimples
To give her an attractive smile.
Obsessed with her image
She runs around with a deep cleavage
Walking like a Queen
With meaningful steps on the catwalk,
She has eyes for no-one.
As she is constantly watching her weight
To avoid looking weird among her rich
And famous friends.

# *Life*

Life
What a difficult word to understand
So much struggle for such a short period of time.

Hanging on her dreams
She realizes life is worth living
No matter how much pain she is going through.

Life has made her stronger.
It is too short to bear grudges and hatred.
It is too precious to waste it in evil actions.

There is no need to be nasty and kill others
Because life on its own is already unbearable.
Everybody has got to go through painful times

So there is no need to inflict pain
And sufferings deliberately on anyone
Whatever the race, culture or color of the skin.

Everything in this world is just an illusion
Life is an obscure mirror impossible to see through
Nothing lasts for ever.

In this life
Better cultivate compassion and generosity.
Wipe all hatred and violence from our hearts.

Just be happy with simple things around us
The songs of a bird or a lovely sunset
Are enough to make life worth living for.

Let us celebrate life
On a new positive note
Of fresh beginning.

Where happiness and hopes
And brotherhood
Are the menus of the day.

Justice
And peace
Become the favorite words of everyone.

A complete new outlook
With powerful meaning
To those ordinary words.

Let us celebrate life
And keep our hopes alive
Because we care for one another.

# *Tears*

Deep inside lays a frozen heart
A creature haunted by a fierce agony.
Tears sparkled like white diamonds
In her tormented eyes.
Her face as white as a ghost
Her limbs paralyzed with fear
Her body lifeless with anguish
As her gaze was lost somewhere
Far away in the world.
So much sobs, signs and pain
For such a vulnerable creature.
Wrapped up in a cold shell of emptiness
Her life is going by.
Days... Years...
Wanting to escape from the harsh realities,
To a dreamy place of her own.
A poor soul who has been kicked
And hit ruthlessly by life.
Days stretched ahead like a never-ending tsunami.
Filled with despair
An emotional void inside a numb body.
Her shoulders hunched,
Her footsteps dragging hopelessly
A dejected figure leaning against a hopeless life.
How many women are out there
Crying in silence and facing the same pain, she wondered.
Futile thoughts
Unhappy images kept her awake
As memories came flooding in.
The sudden death of her beloved mother
Brought even more tears on her cold cheeks.
Everybody can see rain is falling
But nobody can see when a heart is crying.

## (II)

Tears came flooding in her dull eyes,
Which seemed to be like two empty big holes.
She knows she has got nothing to hope for
Nor does she have anything to smile at.
Happiness and peace have been robbed from her for ever.
She thought about her beloved mother.
Her death has left her bewildered.
So many times her world has come crashing at her feet.
And her dreams shattered in pieces.
Her screams of pain lost in the sad puzzle of her life.
Dreams are beautiful and safe.
They help us to keep on struggling
And believe in a better tomorrow.
The aching emptiness dawned on her with every passing day.
Her future devoid of any promises.
Her world like a black cloud hovering on her head.
Her shattered dreams break the dead silence
Reminding her of her despair and loneliness.
Tears came spilling over her cold cheeks.
So many times, her world has come crashing at her feet
Her dreams destroyed
But she still keeps on hoping and struggling.
How long would she live on her broken dreams and hopes?
Carrying her pain through this cruel world
One of her thoughts is:
Dared she hope?
Love had turned into a monster
Tearing her into a helpless piece of nobody.
She wished she was somewhere else.
She wished she could break away from the traumatized experience.
But did she have the courage and the guts to change this situation?
More memories flood in
As painful scenes creep in front of her eyes…
She has believed in love
The eternal and the true one.
She has hoped for a wonderful bliss
Which will last for ever and ever.
How naïve and foolish she was…

## (III)

But the slap she received on her face
Brought her to her senses.
She felt as if she has been slapped
Straight to her heart painfully
And dreadfully.
Tears in the eyes
Pain in the look,
A wounded soul,
A lonely silhouette
Heaviness in the steps
She carried to go through life.
The aching emptiness dawns on her
With every passing day.
Used and abused
In an abusive relationship
She thought he can make her cry for two hours
Or two days
But he cannot make her cry all the times.
He can break her heart
But he cannot break her soul.
He can bend her arm
To make her weak
But he cannot bend her will
To accommodate his furious temper and nastiness.
She has got to believe that she is strong
And capable to take complete control of her own life now.
Trying to be brave
While she craves for happiness and peace,
Waiting such a simple and lonely word
Which cuts deeply like a sword
And which nobody wants to hear
But everybody has got to bear.
After so much waiting for true joys
It has started raining in her heart.
Cold in the dark night
The wind blows her aside
As she stumbles on her twisted fate.
Her thin body wrapped up carelessly
In a worn-out pale blue dress.
Trembled with the fierceness of the pain
Tears came abundantly on her wet face.

## (IV)

Roaming and sauntering through the darkness
One minute she forgot her own pain.
She realizes that there are others also
Who are living in pain and agony,
But nobody cares.
Crying in silence, she can only utter these words…
Oh God! If you cannot give us some joys,
If you refuse to give us some peace
At least, please, grant us the courage
To bear the pain we are going through.
Peace, peace cried a hundred million voices
But this goes unheard.
If only she could change everything to the better,
She would have made the world
A wonderful paradise
For each and everyone.
Peace, love and joy would be shared by all of us….
Children would sing happily God's praises
No pain, no violence and no oppressors.
Is she getting carried away by fairy tales?
She hopes not….

# Mauritius

The plane cruises through the white flake of cloud
Which looks like candy floss,
Hanging above in the open space.
The flight continued undisturbed
While I was lost in the incredible beauty
Of nature filled with warm
And lovely smoke of pure white cloud.
Soon I saw Madagascar,
A huge and long island,
Spreading its shape across the vast panorama.
I looked at the huge size of the wings
Hanging proudly in the air.
A truly amazing technology,
As "Paille-en-Queue" flies across the ocean
To bring me closer to the beautiful island of Mauritius.
Dream destination.
True blue diamond
In the Indian Ocean.
A rainbow nation.
An amazing serene beauty,
A friendly and easy-going people,
A warm smile.
The voice of the co-pilot came as a relief.
The tourists have a huge excited smile
As the plane landed softly and safely on the tarmac.
Leaving the snow and the cold weather behind,
I rushed to the shining sunshine
With joyful trepidation
And excited expectation.
I saw Mahebourg
Standing like a majestic queen ,
Surrounded by her sea-side,
And sparkled like blue-diamond carat.
Truly, she evokes happy and carefree memories.
Passing by Grand-Sable, Petit-Sable
And Bois-des-Amourettes,
The view is truly spectacular.
The blue shining reflects of the sea covers the landscape.

## Magnificent Mauritius

I was stunned in admiration for the breath-taking
And incredible beauty of the entire surrounding.
Fresh fish at "Debarcadere",
The tasty and delicious fruits such as "litchis",
Or 'Longanes" decorate the trees along the roads,
Bringing smiles of delights
And mouth-watering flavors to many of us.
There is an air of joyful expectation
All throughout the island.
Port-Louis is basking in a warm sunshine,
Inviting customers to roam around the shops
And the flea markets of 'Cite Martial".
Some are busy eating their "rotis" or "mine frir",
While others are enjoying their 'alouda glace".
The delicious flavor of the different food filled the air
With temptation and hunger.
Grand-Baie dressed in her blue flowing skirt,
With printed pink flowers like hibiscus
Is ready to flaunt her undoubted beauty
And start dancing on a "sega" beat,
Exhibiting her real color and talent.
Blue-green sparkling sea water surrounds the beaches,
And white soft sand spreading all around.

Wind-surfing through the huge waves can be
The most sensational temptation of the day.
Chamarel
L'ile-aux-cerf
Riambel
Flic-en-Flaq
Pereybere.
Beautiful villas
"Pieds dans l'eau",
Just the kind of paradise someone would admire
And dream about.
Mauritius
Always sweet and fabulous,
Carrying its name with honor
And welcoming each visitor
With a warm sunshine smile.
The truth is :
Fame can burn in flame
Money can disappear in a credit crunch
But your country will always be there
To welcome you.

**delicious longanes decorating the tree**